Inspirational Poems: Decide

Tirzah Sallie

Copyright © 2020 by Tirzah Sallie

All rights reserved. No part of this publication may be reproduced, distributed, or transmitted in any form or by any means, including photocopying, recording, or other electronic or mechanical methods without the prior written permission of the publisher. For permission requests, contact the publisher via email below.

spirationalpoet@gmail.com

Printed in the unite states

ISBN:9798676653347

Dedication

This book is dedicated to everyone that wants to know who Jesus is and desires change in their life.

CONTENTS

1…………………………....The power of Christ

2……………………….I desire to hear God's voice

3………………………… I am the vine; God is the branches

4……………………….Sweet words

5……………………….Every man unto his own shall leave me alone

6……………………….Do not be afraid of terror

7………………Be not wise in your own eyes, be wise in God's eyes

8……………….. White as Snow

9………………………….. What are you standing for?

10……………………………. Dear God, I am giving myself to you

11……………………………. Be bold

12……………………Next Generation

13……. Want to be a World Changer

14…………………………..... What do your heart depend on?

15……………. Dear God, correct me in your word

16……………………………. Be on Bold Moves

17……………………………. Speak Victory and not Defeat

18…………………….............Live for Jesus Christ

19……………………………...Burdens

20……………………………....Who will you serve?

21……………………………..... Die Daily or Kill us forever

22……………………………….. Reveal to Me

23………………What can I do to be a witness to Jesus Christ?

24…………………………………. Motivation to live, love, and laugh

25……………………………..…Peter's Heart of Repentance

26……………………………..…Cover Me

27………………………………….. Motivation

28……………………………..……..... Be like a Flower

29……………………………….…...Arise

30……………………...Hope

31……………………...Going to another level

32……………………………Lord Forgive Me

33……………………………Give more of you

34……………………………The Eye is the lamp of the body

35…………………………….. Shower Down

36…………………………...……Natural vs. Spiritual thoughts

37…………………….....………The Winds of Direction

38……………………………...….. Pride Bye / Jesus Christ is Greater

39…………………………....….. Let us Move

40………………………....….. Your heart

41…………………….………Hello Humbled Pie; Pride Bye

42……………………..………Exploring in Boldness

43.................................…………Speak Life

44.................................…… Just Praise

45....................Everything Counts to me; Counts to Jesus

46..............................…..... I will not settle for less

47................................……What is my inner Beauty?

48.....................…..………Freedom of Cries

49.....................…..………Easier done than said

50...........................…..…Hands to the Plow

51..............................…..I am Capable

52.............................…...Time

The power of Christ

You may not be popular in lights; but make sure you have the power as you travel in this life.

You do not need your name in lights, you just need to surrender yourself to Jesus Christ.

I am not pressed for fame nor fortune; all I desire is to excel in Christ, excel in life, show the world that Jesus is the only way, the truth and life.

All I desire is to be used by Christ, the one who is in control of my life. The true intention that I have in me is to be used by Jesus; the one who saved me, delivered me, and loves me for me.

I desire to hear God's Voice

I really do desire to hear Jesus' voice in life, surrendering all of me and having a peace of mind.

I desire to hear his voice in my life, I have prayed and said, "I give my all to you". I have even prayed for others that really need you.

I have prayed and read from Judges 16:1-31 too.

I am here writing

I am here quiet

I am here waiting

I am here patient

God you are all I need, help me to achieve all my visions in me.

I am still waiting.

I am the Vine; God is the Branches

John 15:5-6

I am the vine, you are the branches, abiding in you because it is far better to bear fruit than to be cast out and burned in the fire.

I am the vine that connects to your branches in you; being used with what I was born and destined to do.

I shall dwell in you; you shall dwell within me so that you can continue to use me. for without you, I can do nothing. Without you I am nothing.

Sweet Words

Psalms 119:103

How sweet are your words to my taste?

Sweeter than honey to my mouth, Yummy!!!!!

Through words of love and encouragement that keep me motivated through every moment of the day.

Moments of love

Moments of Desperation

Moments of sadness and frustration.

Your words keep me lifted like a weight that has been lifted off my shoulders.

Your words keep me lifted through every demon in hell that tried to kill me.

Your words keep me lifted through every offense that has been upon me.

No matter how I feel in my life; your words keep my mind renewed daily.

How sweet are your words to my taste, sweeter than honey to my mouth in every way?

Every Man unto his own, shall leave me alone

John 16:32-33

I am not alone because God is always with me.

Every man that is to his own shall leave me alone.

Walk on

Walk ahead

If you are not for Jesus Christ, just keep walking ahead.

Since Jesus overcame the world, I shall be of good cheer.

In the mist of tribulation in the world remember the father is always with you.

Do not be afraid of terror

Proverbs 24:25-26

Do not be afraid of the terror by night,

your sleep will be sweet, you will be alright.

No matter what terror comes your way,

Your sleep will be sweet anyway.

No matter what terror comes your way,

have confidence in Jesus Christ every day.

Be not wise in your own eyes, be wise in God's eyes

Proverbs 3:7

Be not wise in your own eyes.

Be wise in God's eyes,

Be not wise in your own eyes.

Just realize your eyes see only in the natural, while Jesus sees both naturally and spiritually within you and me.

Do not be wise in your own eyes

but be only wise in God's eyes

White as snow

Isaiah 1:18-20

Though sins are like scarlet, red like crimson.

They shall be white as snow,

As the snow falls from the sky; let your sins be known, let your sins be known to Christ.

If you are willing and obedient; you shall eat the good of the land.

If you refuse and rebel you shall be devoured by the sword" that's so hard to stand.

For the mouth of the Lord has spoken unto you.

Let us all reason together and be willing and obedient

unto his will too.

What are you standing for?

What are you standing for?

I am standing for Jesus Christ for the rest of my life.

What are you standing for?

Standing and willing to spread the word of God to make a difference in this life.

Standing, are you willing?

Willing, are you standing?

I am standing and willing to spread the word of Christ to let others know that Jesus is the only way, the truth, and life.

Dear God, I am giving myself to you

I am giving myself to you in everything I go through.

The opportunities that come in my life, let it be pleasing to you.

The plans that you have destined for me; let my goals match what you have in store for me. Help my creativity develop in you spiritually, so that you can use me.

I give myself to you,

giving you all the praise.

I give myself to you,

each day.

I give myself to you no matter how I feel.

It is your will that allows me to breathe,

It is your will that allows me to speak life within you and me.

It is your will that helps me endure through the pain, dealing with human personalities every day.

Giving myself to you, trusting you with the rest.

Giving myself to you, not worried about no mess.

Be Bold

Be bold, be sold

Be hot, not cold

Be bold, be sold in Christ until the end.

Be bold like a lion that roars out into the atmosphere.

Be bold and stand upon the word of God.

Be bold like a lion that stands up for Christ.

Be bold like a lion that is not afraid to stand up for what is right.

Be bold

Be sold

Be hot

not cold

Be bold in your walk, your talk, and your expressions you give.

Be bold in your style of creativity that others see every day you live.

Be bold around you, Be bold within,

Be bold spreading Jesus,

Be bold till the end.

Next Generation: Motto Poem

The next generation coming to the nation are making a difference in every situation. The birth of a nation refusing the sins of the world and choosing Jesus expectations. We are all here to encourage, love and help each other to make it through this life. We are all here for one purpose and that is getting right with Jesus Christ.

Want to be a world changer?

If you want to be a world changer.

A great effective leader,

It starts with you.

You cannot change others around you.

You can only change you.

It starts with you.

If you desire to be a great influencer with your voice.

Speak words of encouragement that will affect you because before you give a speech to others, you make sure you abide with what you speak too.

Speak to yourself and change what is on the inside of you.

Change anything in yourself that is not like Christ too.

Speak the word of God over your life, so that you will continue to apply the word and live every day in perfecting Christ.

Changing for the better in your life.

Changing the inside that is so fleshly into changing spiritually in Jesus Christ.

If you want to be a world changer follow Jesus Christ, he knows what is in store for your wonderful life.

What does your heart depend on?

This poem was inspired by Marcus Rodger's YouTube video called: "Beware of Doctrines of Devils and Seducing spirits"

Faith

Love

Humiliation

Sin

Condemnation

Situation

Which one does your heart depend on?

Do you depend on God's standard or the devil's standard in your life?

Do you depend on your feelings or do you operate by faith which is more pleasing to Christ?

Once that line comes off the coast in this life, separating the wheat and the tear, it will really show who is bold for Christ.

Which one does your heart depend on?

The devil's standard or God's standards which are more pleasing to Christ.

Dear God, correct me in your word

2 Timothy 3:16-17

Dear God,

correct me in your word and give me instructions for my purpose.

Instruction

Direction

Connection

Protection

Get me connected to the right people in my life.

Direct me to what path you desire for me to take according to your will in this life. Encamp your angels and protection over your children in the Kingdom of Christ.

Encamp your angels and protection over the lost souls upon this earth to come to you with surrendering hearts.

Allow them to have a made-up mind to live only just for you.

Be on Bold Moves

Be beautiful like a butterfly.

Soar like an eagle in the sky.

Roar like a lion when words are speaking out my mouth.

Be on bold moves and have great determination within you.

Be on bold moves to be excellent in Jesus Christ too.

I am a butterfly.

I soar within Christ,

I roar with great power in my words when I speak life.

I am everything that God has destined in me.

I am a vessel in Christ that is willing to sacrifice

everything in me.

Speak Victory and not Defeat

In so many paths of life, so many people do not realize that their hardships are what makes them stronger.

Some people commit suicide and discourage themselves because of how hard their situations are. You must realize that your hardships build you up like a military going through war.

In every situation that you go through speak victory and not defeat. Do not allow defeat to overcome the victory.

Remember Jesus Christ is eternally within you and me. He will never leave you nor forsake you. He is always right there by your side in your life.

Speak victory and not defeat, God is eternally within you and me.

Speak victory to your feet.

Speak victory to your body.

Speak victory to your brain.

Speak victory to your hands.

Speak victory to your grades.

Speak victory to your job.

Speak victory to your attitude.

Speak victory to yourself to be right. Speak victory to yourself and say that I can do all things through Christ.

Speak victory.

Live for Jesus Christ

Everyone will go to eternity; just know that your eternity is based on how you are living now.

Live for Christ.

Do not live for yourself.

Live for Christ Living holy might be challenging but it is worth your whole life.

Live for Jesus Christ.

I went through for three days because my grandfather died. Did a lot of thinking and said to myself, "Life Moves On"? I thought about Jesus of how he rose on the third day. Since He rose on the third day; I moved on.

Continue to stay encouraged and live according to God's purpose and plan for your life. Keep smiling because when you choose Jesus Christ everything will be alright.

Burdens

Burdens drag, suck, and ruin you like a raisin in the sun that runs out of moisture.

Release it all to God and he will bring you through.

How can you say you are free and still saying that all things are not working well for you?

You really must trust God in your life so that he can guide you on what you need to do.

Remember that all things will work well for those who love Christ.

Release your burdens to Jesus in your life. He will lead and guide you for the rest of your life.

Never give-up in whatever situation you go through

because with Christ all things will work together just

for you.

Who will you serve?

Giving all myself to Jesus in everything that I go through. Not ashamed to say that I really love you.

Wondering, why are people swaying left and right?

Choose a path.

What do you want to do?

Jesus gave you freedom of choice; he will not force anything on you.

We are living in the last days,

What do you want to do?

We do not have much time on this earth.

Decide, which one are you going to serve?

You only serve one master.

Die Daily or Kill us forever

Die daily or kill us Forever

Die Daily or kill us forever

The more you die in your flesh

The more you die, the more blessed.

The less you die in your flesh,

The less you die, the less you are blessed.

Go into what God has for you,

Do not do what you want to do.

The way you live in this world determines where you will be.

Live for Christ and you will be with him for eternity.

Be where God wants you to be

Do not be where you want to be.

God knows your future in your life

So please die daily in the flesh and

live spiritually according to Jesus Christ.

Lord, reveal to me

Lord, reveal to me what you see in me.

Reveal to me what you see spiritually so that I can change within me.

Reveal to me what you see in every industry.

Help me to be awake.

Awake in my spirit.

Awake in my life.

Awake.

It is all in God's hand.

It is all in his plan.

He wants us to awake now,

It is getting close to the end.

What can I do to be a witness to Jesus Christ?

What can I do to be a witness for you?

Help me to understand mentally and spiritually in you.

What can I do to be a witness for you?

Help me to understand the things of you.

Help me to understand what to do in your kingdom too.

It is all about living right unto God no matter what your going through. Releasing your issues unto him, not ashamed to say that I love you.

What I can do to be a witness to Jesus Christ is give him all my life, ask for forgiveness for what you have done that was not right, and let him take control and go along with the ride.

Get baptized in Jesus name; no other name, no other name I know.

Seek God's face for the Holy Ghost and live for Jesus Christ 100%.

Motivation to live, love, and laugh

Motivation within habitation trying to stay encouraged through every situation.

Not ashamed of my past; moving on with inspiration, without no hesitation, being determined to reach my destination.

Live, Love, Laugh

Live, Love, Laugh

Live

Live through the process in your life.

Love others that treat you wrong or right.

Laugh in your hard times that you go through and encourage others and yourself in everything that you do.

Live in your purpose that God has destined for you.

Do not deny the call, accept the calling in your life too.

Not serving with your own will but with God's recognition.

Motivation within habitation trying to stay encouraged through every situation.

Not ashamed of my past; moving on with inspiration, without no

hesitation, being determined to reach my lovely destination.

Peter's Heart of Repentance

Expressing my heart of repentance upon you.

I denied you once, twice, three times. Lord forgive me too.

Expressing my heart of repentance upon you.

Lord forgive me for being so ashamed of you.

How could I let this be?

How could I deny you?

My Savior, the one who died for me.

I am such a mess right now.

Lord forgive me for being so ashamed of you.

I am not perfect in my life, help me to be perfect in you.

Releasing my heart of repentance upon you.

Renewing my mind in your words too.

Help me to be refreshed through your words and be bold in you.

Expressing my heart of repentance upon you.

Cover Me

Cover me from the crown of my head to the souls of my feet. Cover me from the crown of my head to the souls of my feet. God is with you, he will protect you everywhere you go, God will protect you through your trials and tribulations. God will always protect you everywhere you go, he will keep you safe, he will not let you go he will be there always. God will protect you; he is with you everywhere you go. He will love you; he will be there for you no matter what. Cover me from the crown of my head to the souls of my feet. Cover me from the crown of my head to the souls of my feet.

Motivation

Motivation within habitation trying to stay encouraged through every situation.

Not ashamed of my past; moving on with inspiration. Without no hesitation, being determined to reach my destination.

Within this destination, learn to take situations with consideration.

Serving people with the act of God rather than their own ambition.

Not serving with your own will but with God's recognition.

Your situation is based on your observation unless your mentality is full of frustration.

Do not let your frustration take control of your situation.

So, you can be successful in your future destination.

Always have someone that cares about your heart; never have someone that will shoot you with darts.

Questioning God within your own frustration?

Seek God's face more and more; he will relieve you from your crazy situation.

Once you have submitted yourself to Christ; let him control the wheel of your life.

He knows what beholds in your future; just trust him.

No questions asked, just seek him.

In fact, just believe him.

Be like a Flower

A flower is a beautiful object that represents a woman's beauty; the leaf represents the body.

A flower withers from the weather and blossoms when the sun comes up. Humans get destroyed from drugs and rise when they decide they want to change.

A flower comes in different types of colors, just like human beings.

Stay strong and do not let your troubles take over you.

Be like a flower that is confident and feels good about itself too.

Be like a flower that stands up and does not care what other people say.

Be like a flower that encourages others every day.

Arise

Arise through my testimony,

Arise through my pain.

Arise through every situation,

no matter the gain.

Building blocks breaking through every tear,

crying out for help when you feel like God is not near.

You know what, you will make it through your pain because Jesus will break through every chain no matter the gain.

Slaves go to the other side of freedom getting out from what they were held captive for; never settle for less.

Always strive for what Jesus has for you.

Strive for excellence.

<u>Hope</u>

In life there is always hope for you no matter what you are going through.

Just know that during your situation Jesus will always make away for you.

Stay encouraged in Jesus because he has a purpose for you.

There is always hope for each one of you.

Never think to yourself, you are worthless because of the momentarily situations that you go through.

Let go and let God, so he can bring you through.

Stay encouraged, you are full of hope in your life.

Going to another level

I am going to another level in my life.

I am going to another place.

Not ashamed to say that God is going to open doors for me.

Not going to let no one stop me from being successful in Christ.

I am going to another level in my life, putting God first in spite.

No matter what happens in my life.

I am going to give God all the praise.

No matter where I am in this life.

I am going to another level.

I am going to another place.

No matter what happens to me, with Jesus all things will work together for me.

I am going to another level.

Lord Forgive Me

Lord, forgive me if I have done anything that was not like you.

Please forgive me for being so selfish to you.

Forgive me,

please forgive me.

Help me to rely only on you and trust in your will, not mine.

Lord, keep me from my flesh that goes against you. Help me to walk in my spiritual man in you.

Lord, help me.

Help me to be more like you.

Guide me to where you want me to be in you.

Give more of you

Give Jesus everything,

give him more of you.

Never give up on him because

he first loved you.

Love shows and speaks; sharing the testimony of others that is going through.

Never be ashamed of what God has given you because he has called you out from a chosen few to make a difference around you.

Be real, be you, and be who God called you to be in his kingdom too. Be the person that is not ashamed to encourage others in Jesus name. This world has no hope without him each day.

Spread your testimonies and make a difference.

Be you, there is only one you.

No one can do you like you.

Do not be ashamed of who you are on the inside.

Appreciate who you are and love you for you.

Give Jesus more of you so you can be used.

Give him more of you.

The Eye is the lamp of the body

Matthew 6:22-24

Help me to distinguish what is bad from good.

Help me to discern boldly in your name as I should.

The eye is the lamp of the body which reveals who you are from the inside. The true intentions of your heart matters in people's lives.

The eye-draws people

The heart- reveals

The body-shows who we truly represent.

The eyes draw people to you. The heart reveals who they are when they speak out their mouth. The body shows what they will do in their true intentions of you.

Help me to discern boldly in your name as I should in you.

Bold when I am speaking; when I am silent; in my stature in my stand in you. Bold when I am looking at the right place at the right time.

Discern the situation when I drive in the car. Discern the situation when I look from afar. Discern boldly in everything in my life to live in Christ, speak life. Discern when things are going right.

Discern when things are going wrong. Discern everything around me in Christ. Help me to discern whats around me in this life. amen.

Shower Down

Shower down your blessings on your people.

Rain down your mercy on us.

Transform our lives through your word to dwell

within me spiritually not in the flesh.

Shower down your blessings on your people.

Rain down your mercy on us.

Transform our lives through the word to dwell

within me spiritually; not the flesh.

Walking into my new self at last,

leaving the old me in the past.

Natural vs. Spiritual thought

Natural thoughts of Life

You do what you want to do. You do what you got to do. You do what you want to do. You got to follow patterns in your desire through your actions. You got to follow through.

Spiritual thoughts of life

You do what God wants you to do. You must follow pattern in his will he has for you. You got to follow through In this life that we live, we choose what we want to do, but in this life that we live we must seek God's face and ask, "What shall I do?"

You do what God tells you to do in your life.

Go ahead and follow the pattern that he has instore for your life. He knows what is in store for you. Do not go ahead and do what you want to do.

You got to follow pattern in what Jesus has in store for you.

Do you want to go to heaven?

Do you want to go to heaven in your life?

Do you want to be in the New Jerusalem?

where Jesus Christ is in spite?

Think it through, think it through say yes to heaven; say no to hell in your life.

The Winds of Direction

Ecclesiastes 11:5

Winds of direction can be whatever is pulling you towards your destiny. God's direction calling you where you are supposed to be at the right place at the right time.

Follow Jesus' still small voice; the holy ghost winds which pushes you closer to reach your full potential in your life.

The winds that blow during the day.

The winds that blow during the night.

Whispering direction from every move in your life.

Winds of careers and winds of others in your life.

Follow God's still small voice and let the holy ghost blow you

in your right direction in your life. The winds of direction that you

hear in your ears. The winds of direction that God tells you near and near. Winds of people that try to get you off track in life.

The wind of the holy ghost puts you at the right place at the right time. As the wind blows Jesus know what is in store for your life. Just follow his still small voice and let God lead you in the right direction in your life. As the wind blows, you go.

As the wind blows, Jesus knows your life. Even without the wind blowing, Jesus can tell you what is next for your life.

Pride Bye

Proverbs 21:25

A proud and haughty man-

Scoffer is his name; He acts with arrogant

pride. That is so insane.

How can you be filled with pride?

Please put that aside, Pride bye!

Pride go to the side or be like Satan

that was full of pride. Guess where that got him?

answer: thrown out the sky.

Pride bye.

Jesus Christ is Greater

Proverbs 22:2

The rich and the poor have this in common,

the Lord is the maker of them all.

So please, please!! stop telling everybody that you are better

than others because Jesus Christ is greater

than all.

Let us Move

Do not let anyone tell you what you cannot do. You can do all things through Christ which strengthens you.

Do not let no one tell you what you cannot do. I can do all things through Christ which strengthens me too.

You are so powerful and wonderful in God's eyes, let us all move according to Jesus Christ.

Let us move

Let us move

Let us move

Let us move in God too.

Let us move,

Move, move, move

let us move in God's will too. Let us move according to our purpose in our life. Do not let no one tell you what you cannot do. You can do all things through Christ which strengthens you.

Do not let no one tell you what you cannot do. You can do all things through Christ which strengthens you.

(3x) move

Let us operate in the spirit, not the flesh.

Let us operate in the spirit, not the flesh.

Let us move

Your heart

Let your heart be filled with good intentions as you live this life. Being content with having a pure heart in Christ.

Pure intentions that you strive for everyday in your life.

Focus to have a heart for Jesus in life because he knows where your heart is.

Your heart is beating with purpose, beating with change, and beating for every soul that needs Jesus Christ in their life.

Your heart is beating with purpose and beating with change.

Your heart is striving for purity in Christ; I hope you are striving for the same. Continue to perfect your spiritual beings in life by loving one another in Jesus Christ.

Hello Humble Pie; Pride Goodbye

Pride Bye, Pride Bye

Go to the side.

Pride bye, Pride bye

Hello Humble pie, Hello Humble pie

Pride goodbye.

Let us keep on moving in this life.

Do not care what others say about you in your life. Just keep in your mind, pride bye. I am going to stay high where Jesus is in the sky.

Pride bye, pride bye

Hello Humble pie

Staying humble is the greatest thing in your life because Jesus died for you and me in this life. He is the one who gave you life. So, let us stop all that (all that) pride. He is the one who provides.

Walk humbly in your life and just do what God has assigned for you. Let Jesus move in your life and trust God in every move you make in life.

Pride bye, Hello Humble pie, pride bye

Stay on the humble side.

Exploring in Boldness

Boldly going, boldly exploring going to get the pieces of me.

Boldly going out to where God wants me to be.

Boldly going, boldly exploring by doing Jesus will in my life.

Building on bold moves to where God has for me to be as I live life.

Being bold by exploring by faith not by sight.

Exploring boldly getting the pieces of me in the world that God has created for me in this life.

Trust God with your creativity he has given you and explore boldly in your gifts and do not be ashamed of Jesus Christ.

Explore boldly spiritually in your life and let Jesus take over by sacrificing the flesh and operating in the spirit in your life.

Explore in Boldness and let Jesus guide you in your life.

Speak Life

Speak life on the roaming souls that are lost and do not know Jesus Christ. For those who know Jesus, allow them to have the desire to live a life that is for you; Not just saying "I LOVE THE LORD".

Allow their lifestyle to show you,

to show you that their heart is for you.

Show you that they are sold out for you.

speak life, speak life, speak life

to your brain to have a renewed mind in Christ.

Always speak life to your heart beating regularly.

I speak life to your limbs, hands, and feet to praise God no matter what you go through. I speak life to your surroundings; God's protection over you. Encamping angels around you from the cunning plans that the devil has planned for you.

You have overcome in your life.

You have the victory.

Speak life over yourself because your words are powerful within you and me. I speak life for those who are for you not against you. Speaking life in your spiritual being to come alive; to be used in Jesus in everything that you do.

I speak life to your family to be saved in Jesus Christ. Speaking life to your eyes to see spiritually while living naturally in this life. Speaking to your life to remind you that Jesus is the only way, the truth, and the life.

Just Praise

Just praise instead of holding things within yourself. Be determined for what God has for you.

Praise and work on getting yourself right with Jesus Christ.

You do not know what others have been through to get to their goal in life.

You do not know what others have been through so just find your purpose in Jesus Christ. Be excited for people in life.

Your time is coming. Let God get all the glory in life. No matter how you feel inside; just know that God will provide for you.

No matter how you feel inside; release your issues to Jesus and he will come through for you.

Releasing, renewing, and refreshing yourself in Christ.

Deal with your situations and overcome everything in life. Just be happy while you go through the processes of life.

Just Praise.

Everything counts to me: Counts to Jesus

Everything that counts to me; counts to Jesus

in what you do and say.

Everything counts to me; counts to Jesus.

Let us live according to Jesus today.

Let us live according to our purpose in life and not the enticement

of our flesh that tries to overcome us in life.

Everything that counts to me; counts to Jesus

in what we do and say.

Everything that counts to me; counts to Jesus.

Let us live according to our purpose in Jesus Christ.

Start today, tomorrow is not promised to you in your life.

I will not settle for less

I will not settle for less. I will not settle for mess.

I will not settle for anything that will keep me in distress.

Keep this in your mind; forget mess.

Strive for better than less.

Strive for Jesus, the one who knows your future in your life.

I will not settle for mess because I am fearfully and wonderfully made in God's eyes.

I will reach my full potential in life.

I will reach my full potential in Jesus Christ.

I will reach my full potential in my desires that will make a difference in this life.

I will not settle. I will strive for better in Jesus Christ.

What is my inner Beauty?

Dear Lord,

I know your beauty is beautiful within me.

Your guidance in your word leads me.

What is my inner beauty?

I am a pure gem that encourages others in my life.

All I desire is you in my life.

What is my inner beauty?

Your holiness is beautiful inside of me; show and reveal to me my inner beauty.

You see me in your perspective up above through the blood of Jesus I am fully loved.

Jesus you are the beauty of holiness.

Freedom of Cries

Freedom of Cries.

Releasing the pain in your life.

Freedom of Cries releasing from your eyes; tears of pain.

Releasing tears of freedom from the inside out.

Crying when you are going through like a baby that cries

for love and hunger as they develop every day in their life.

Freedom of cries, releasing the pain from the inside out day and night.

Freedom, freedom of cries

Freedom, feeling release from your eyes.

Freedom, freedom of cries releasing the pain from your eyes.

Releasing joy, sadness, and frustration in your life.

You cannot keep things in yourself; you got to express yourself externally in your life.

Releasing freedom each day by releasing it to Jesus Christ today.

He can help you with everything in your life. Release it to God

because he can set you free and give you eternal life.

Easier done than said

So many people say it the other way. Why not switch it and speak life today?

Easier done than said.

Let us get it done; less talking. Easier done than said so we can make it to our destiny and not wish upon our future instead.

Live according to Jesus standards in your life; it may seem hard because of the way people present things in your life.

Easier done than said. The world says, "easier said than done."

I even say it in my life, it is all about your mental mind.

Easier done than said.

When you believe in Jesus Christ; the one who spoke life.

He spoke words into existence and blew through your

Nostrils so that you can live your destined life.

Speak words of life like, "easier done than said."

Speak life like Jesus Christ did in the beginning

of this life.

You can do all things through Jesus Christ.

Speak life. Believe.

You will be alright.

Hands to the Plow

Ecclesiastes 9:10

Whatever your hands find to do,

do it with all your might; for

there is no work, or device or knowledge

or wisdom in the grave of life.

Open your hands and put it to the plow like a person working their hands upon a cow to get milk.

Oh wow; a cow

Let us put our hands to the plow.

Hands nurture, create, and move along when we talk; that is great.

Let us put our hands to the plow.

Let us put our hands to the plow like we get milk from a cow.

Let us get it done.

We have already won.

Let us get it done.

We won.

I am Capable

I am capable and able to do what I am supposed to do.

I am capable and able to prosper all I set my hands to.

I am capable and able to retain information that is new.

I am capable to endure through this life in everything I do.

I am capable of fighting and speaking up in life.

I am capable to do what I am created to do.

I will get back up to succeed.

I will be the best that I can be.

I can do all things through Christ which strengthens me.

I can make a difference and spread the gospel till

the end of time in the community.

___Time___

Time is an essence You cannot get it back

Time is an essence. You got to stay on track

Time is an essence; you will not get back.

So, let us stay on track to what God has for us in life.

We cannot keep looking back because God is going forward in our lives.

Time t-t-t-time

Time t-t-t-time

We are running out of time.

Let us get ourselves right with Jesus Christ because he is the reason why we live purposefully in our life.

We are running out of time. So, let us move in purpose and flow in Jesus Christ.

time t-t-t-time

Time is an essence. You cannot get it back.

Time is an essence. You got to stay on track. Time is essence, you will not get back. So, let us stay on track to what God has for us in life.

Let us live according to Jesus Christ.

Looking forward to where Jesus is moving in our life.

Time is moving. Let us keep our minds on the one who gave us life.

Acknowledgments

I would like to first thank Jesus Christ for the words of encouragement he has given me to help me in my life to get through my challenging moments.

I thank my family and friends that prayed and encouraged me to write and not give up.

Grandma Ingrid-Thank you for your love and prayers. You are the best.

Mom- thank you for sending poems of encouragement to me to keep me lifted and loving me unconditionally.

Dad- Thank you for your provision and love when I needed you the most.

Aunt Lisa - Thank you for allowing God to use you in my life to encourage me at my lowest hour and praying with me.

Betty Tyler (Spiritual Godmother)-Thank you for praying for me, encouraging me, and holding me accountable all around spiritually. You are truly blessed and your healed in Jesus name.

Shekinah B. -Thank you for encouraging me in my life. When I see you strive for your goals with Jesus in your life; it inspires me to keep being creative and not give up. Love you girl.

God dad (Juanita and Cleveland Glenn)- Thank you both for your wonderful words of encouragement.

Charles Wright-Thank you for encouraging, praying, and telling me that the world is my oyster.

Henrietta Holiday- Thank you for your great encouragement in every conversation we had together on the phone. You are a powerful woman full of greatness. Continue to smile and be

merry. Thank you for allowing God to use you.

Shirley Thompson- Thank you for encouraging, praying, and keeping me uplifted.

Levada Whitfield-Thank you for holding me accountable.

ABOUT THE AUTHOR

Tirzah Sallie is a motivational author who desires to inspire others through her testimonies and words of encouragement. She started to write back in September 2006 when her cousin died expressing her words on paper of how she felt. Her purpose in writing poetry is to express her love for Jesus Christ and how far she has come because of God's grace and mercy in her life. As she grows in her relationship with Jesus, she learns that no matter how hard the world tries to bring you down; continue to speak words of life to yourself in Jesus name and know that God will always be by your side with angels protecting you as you live with purpose.

Made in the USA
Middletown, DE
08 May 2023